SHUFFLE

THE RISE OF KABELO DLAMINi

While every precaution has been taken in the preparation of this book, the publisher assumes no responsibility for errors or omissions, or for damages resulting from the use of the information contained herein.

SHUFFLE: THE RISE OF KABELO DLAMINI

First edition. February 28, 2025.

Copyright © 2025 Sibusiso Anthon Mkhwanazi.

ISBN: 979-8227317186

Written by Sibusiso Anthon Mkhwanazi.

Also by Sibusiso Anthon Mkhwanazi

Million-Dollar Decade
Resilience Beyond Pain
Resonance Of Hope
Cheating hearts to true love
The Dream Builders Of Daveyton
Before the Bible
Ink and Imagination
Becoming A Millionaire In South Africa
Leaders of the World
Mining In Africa
Origins of Language and Civilization
Vita Nova Centre
Sisters of A cursed bloodline
Witchcraft in Africa
Ghosts of the golden city
Connected Hearts
Lost in Tokyo found in you
A man of many homes
Shuffle: The Rise of Kabelo Dlamini

Table of Contents

Shuffle: The Rise of Kabelo Dlamini 1
Dedication 3
Introduction 5
Chapter 1: The Streets of Daveyton 7
Chapter 2: Dreams of Greatness 9
Chapter 3: Mentors and Role Models 13
Chapter 4: First Breakthrough 17
Chapter 5: The Celtic Opportunity 21
Chapter 6: Promotion to the First Team 25
Chapter 7: Hard Work Pays Off 31
Chapter 8: The Call from Orlando Pirates 35
Chapter 9: Making His Mark at Pirates 39
Chapter 10: The Zinnbauer Era 43
Chapter 11: Pursuing National Dreams 47
Chapter 12: Champions League Aspirations 51
Chapter 13: Loyalty to the Buccaneers 57
Chapter 14: Overcoming Adversity and Staying Focused 63
Chapter 15: The Zinnbauer Era and Personal Growth 69
Chapter 16: The Road to Continental Glory 75
Chapter 17: The Legacy of a Buccaneer 81
Chapter 18: The Legacy in the Making 87
Chapter 19: The Road Still to Travel 89
Book Description 95

Written by
SIBUSISO ANTHON MKHWANAZI

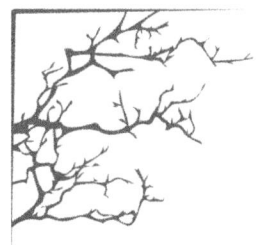

Dedication

To the streets of Daveyton,
where dreams are born and resilience is forged.
To my family, for their unwavering support and sacrifices,
your love has been my greatest motivation.
To every coach, teammate, and mentor who believed in me,
your guidance shaped the player and person I am today.
And to every young boy and girl chasing a dream,
may my journey remind you that nothing is impossible with hard work, discipline, and faith.
This is for you.

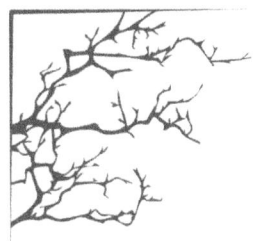

Introduction

Every great journey begins with a single step. For Kabelo Dlamini, his journey from the dusty streets of Daveyton to the glittering lights of professional football was one of grit, determination, and unshakable belief in his dreams. Born into a township bursting with raw talent and potential, Kabelo grew up surrounded by the rhythm of life—vivid, challenging, and inspiring. His story is not just about football; it's about the power of perseverance and the pursuit of excellence against all odds.

Kabelo's rise to stardom is a tale rooted in humble beginnings. In a community where opportunities were scarce and challenges abundant, his love for the beautiful game became a lifeline. Football was more than a sport; it was a language, a culture, and for Kabelo, a beacon of hope. His skill, determination, and work ethic earned him the nickname "Shuffle," a reflection of his electrifying footwork and unique style of play.

The nickname "Shuffle" embodies Kabelo's essence as a player—quick, creative, and unpredictable. It's a moniker that represents his ability to navigate the field with flair, leaving defenders guessing and fans in awe. To many, it's just a nickname, but to Kabelo, it's a testament to his artistry and the countless hours he spent perfecting his craft on the streets of Daveyton.

This book is a celebration of Kabelo's journey—a young boy from Ekasi with dreams larger than life. It's a story of resilience, family, community, and the relentless pursuit of greatness. As we delve into the chapters of his life, you'll witness the trials, triumphs, and lessons that shaped Kabelo Dlamini into the player and person he is today.

Welcome to the story of "Shuffle," a rising star whose journey has only just begun.

Chapter 1: The Streets of Daveyton

Life in Daveyton: Community, Culture, and Challenges

Daveyton, a vibrant township on the eastern outskirts of Johannesburg, is a place brimming with life, culture, and resilience. Known for its close-knit community and a deep love for football, the streets of Daveyton are more than just pathways—they are stages where dreams are born and talent flourishes. The township pulses with a rhythm of camaraderie and survival, where neighbors look out for each other and everyone shares in the hardships and joys of daily life.

Amidst the challenges of limited resources and economic hardships, Daveyton's residents hold onto hope and pride. The township has a rich tradition of producing remarkable talent, from musicians and artists to footballers who make their mark on the national stage. This environment fosters resilience, creativity, and a relentless determination to rise above circumstances.

Early Influences: Family, Friends, and Local Heroes

For Kabelo Dlamini, family was the cornerstone of his upbringing. Raised in a humble home, his parents instilled in him the values of discipline and hard work. Though financial struggles were a constant reality, Kabelo's parents ensured that their children were grounded and focused on their dreams.

In the streets of Daveyton, Kabelo found inspiration from local legends like Jabu "Shuffle" Mahlangu, whose exploits on the field brought pride to the township. Watching these players gave Kabelo a sense of what was possible and fueled his aspirations to follow in their footsteps. His friends, too, played a pivotal role in his early journey. Together, they formed makeshift teams, using stones for goalposts and playing with tattered balls. These moments were not just about football—they were about forging bonds, sharing dreams, and learning life lessons.

Kabelo's First Steps in Football

Kabelo's passion for football ignited at a young age. The streets were his first playground, and the local tournaments became his proving ground. Barefoot and determined, he showcased his skills, often dazzling older players with his quick feet and clever moves. Kabelo's natural talent and charisma on the field earned him the attention of local coaches, who saw his potential and encouraged him to take his passion more seriously.

Street football taught Kabelo invaluable lessons—how to adapt, think on his feet, and never back down from a challenge. These games were fast-paced and unforgiving, mirroring the realities of life in Daveyton. Yet, they were also filled with joy and camaraderie, laying the foundation for the player Kabelo would become.

As Kabelo began to excel in local tournaments, his reputation grew. People started to refer to him as "Shuffle," likening his flair and agility to the great Jabu Mahlangu. This nickname would become a symbol of Kabelo's identity, representing not only his skill but also the dreams and pride of Daveyton.

From those dusty streets to the fields of professional football, Kabelo Dlamini's journey began here—in the heart of Daveyton, where talent and determination collide to create greatness.

Chapter 2: Dreams of Greatness

Joining Local Football Clubs and Discovering His Passion

As Kabelo Dlamini grew, his passion for football became undeniable. What started as a pastime in the streets of Daveyton evolved into a serious pursuit when he joined local football clubs. These clubs were more than just teams—they were schools of discipline, resilience, and teamwork. Kabelo's first foray into organized football came through a neighborhood club, where he quickly stood out for his technical skills, creativity, and sharp instincts.

Every match became an opportunity for Kabelo to prove himself, and every training session was a chance to refine his abilities. Coaches recognized his potential and often encouraged him to play with older age groups, challenging him to push his limits. It was during these formative years that Kabelo realized football was more than a hobby—it was his calling.

His love for the game only deepened as he watched televised matches of his idols, players like Benni McCarthy and Teko Modise. Kabelo began to emulate their moves, blending their techniques with his unique style. These moments solidified his dream of playing professional football, igniting an ambition that would drive him through life's toughest moments.

The Sacrifices His Family Made to Support His Budding Talent

Behind Kabelo's blossoming career was a family that believed in his dreams. Despite their limited means, his parents and siblings went to great lengths to support his passion. Buying football boots or paying club fees often meant sacrificing other necessities, yet his family never wavered in their commitment.

Kabelo's mother, a pillar of strength, would work long hours to ensure he had the basics needed to train and play. His father, though often stretched thin by financial constraints, encouraged Kabelo to stay focused and never lose sight of his goals. Even his siblings played their part, stepping in to cover chores or sharing their allowances to fund his football endeavors.

The sacrifices were not always easy. Kabelo's family faced criticism from neighbors who questioned the practicality of supporting a football dream in a community where many aspired to more traditional careers. Yet, their unwavering belief in Kabelo's potential kept them resolute. For Kabelo, this support became a source of motivation. Knowing his family had his back pushed him to work harder, ensuring their sacrifices were not in vain.

Challenges of Balancing School, Football, and Home Responsibilities

Despite his growing talent, Kabelo's journey was far from smooth. Balancing school, football, and home responsibilities proved to be a monumental task. His days were grueling—early morning chores, long hours at school, afternoon training sessions, and late nights studying. There were times when exhaustion threatened to overwhelm him, but Kabelo's determination kept him going.

School was not just an academic challenge; it was also a social one. Many of Kabelo's peers struggled to understand his commitment to football, often teasing him for missing outings or failing to keep up with the latest trends. Teachers, too, were skeptical of his ambitions, urging him to focus on his studies rather than chasing what they saw as an unrealistic dream.

At home, Kabelo carried his share of responsibilities. From fetching water to helping care for younger siblings, he contributed to the family's daily life. These tasks, though demanding, taught him the value of hard work and humility. They also instilled in him a deep sense of gratitude for his parents, whose tireless efforts made his journey possible.

Football, however, remained his sanctuary. On the pitch, Kabelo could escape the pressures of life and express himself freely. The game became a source of joy and a reminder of what he was working toward.

Emerging Determination and Drive

Through these challenges, Kabelo developed a resilience that would define his career. He learned to prioritize, often sacrificing sleep or leisure to meet his commitments. He also began to understand the importance of discipline, recognizing that success required more than talent—it demanded effort, focus, and perseverance.

Kabelo's story during this period is a testament to the power of dreams and the sacrifices they often require. It highlights the role of family, community, and an unyielding drive in overcoming adversity. For Kabelo, these years were not just about football—they were about laying the foundation for a future where greatness was not just a dream but a destiny waiting to be fulfilled.

Chapter 3: Mentors and Role Models

Key Figures Who Shaped His Career

Every great player has a support system of individuals who see potential before it's realized, offering guidance and inspiration. For Kabelo Dlamini, these mentors were the architects of his success, shaping his career at pivotal moments. From community coaches to professional role models, their influence played a crucial role in his development.

One of the earliest figures to believe in Kabelo was Coach Thami, who managed a local club in Daveyton. Coach Thami's training sessions were rigorous, designed to instill discipline and sharpen technical skills. He taught Kabelo to respect the game by arriving early, maintaining physical fitness, and understanding the importance of teamwork. Coach Thami often reminded his players, "Talent will open doors, but discipline will keep them open." This philosophy became a cornerstone of Kabelo's journey.

Another influential figure was Jabu "Shuffle" Mahlangu, the Daveyton-born legend who had made it big in South African football. Seeing someone from his community achieve greatness ignited a spark in Kabelo. Jabu's electrifying style of play inspired Kabelo to adopt a flair that later became his signature.

Lessons Learned from Siyangaphi and Musa Nyatama

As Kabelo's career progressed, he encountered mentors like Siyangaphi and Musa Nyatama, both of whom left an indelible mark on his journey. Siyangaphi, a seasoned coach, had a knack for identifying young talent and nurturing it. His approach went beyond technical training—he focused on developing mental toughness and emotional intelligence.

Siyangaphi's sessions were intense, often pushing players to their limits. Kabelo remembers one particular moment when he was exhausted and ready to quit a grueling drill. Siyangaphi pulled him aside and said, "If you quit here, you'll quit everywhere else in life. Push through." That lesson stayed with Kabelo, teaching him the value of perseverance, especially in high-pressure situations.

Musa Nyatama, a professional player Kabelo admired, played a different role in his life. As a mentor, Musa offered practical advice on navigating the challenges of professional football. He shared insights about handling fame, managing finances, and staying grounded amidst success.

One of Musa's most valuable lessons was the importance of humility. "Football is a short career," Musa often said. "Treat everyone with respect because your legacy isn't just about what you do on the field—it's about how you impact others off it." Kabelo took this wisdom to heart, ensuring he remained approachable and supportive, especially to younger players.

How Mentorship Built His Discipline and Work Ethic

The cumulative influence of his mentors transformed Kabelo into a disciplined and hardworking individual. Under their guidance, he learned to set goals and create actionable plans to achieve them. He began waking up earlier to fit in extra training sessions, reviewing his performances critically to identify areas for improvement, and studying the playing styles of football greats to refine his technique.

Discipline became Kabelo's competitive edge. While many players relied solely on natural talent, Kabelo's work ethic set him apart. He would often stay behind after training to practice free kicks or improve his dribbling skills. These moments of extra effort were the direct result of his mentors' teachings.

His mentors also emphasized the importance of mental preparation. They taught him how to handle criticism, recover from mistakes, and stay focused during matches. Kabelo's ability to maintain composure under pressure became one of his defining traits, earning him the respect of teammates and coaches alike.

The Broader Impact of Role Models

Mentorship didn't just shape Kabelo's football career—it influenced his character. Through his mentors, he learned the value of giving back and lifting others as he climbed. He began to mentor younger players in his community, sharing the lessons he had learned and encouraging them to pursue their dreams.

For Kabelo, mentorship was more than a relationship; it was a lifeline. It gave him the tools to navigate challenges, the confidence to chase greatness, and the vision to inspire others. As he reflected on his journey, Kabelo realized that the most important thing his mentors had given him wasn't advice or training—it was belief. Their faith in his potential became the foundation on which he built his dreams.

In the years to come, Kabelo would honor his mentors by paying their lessons forward, ensuring that their influence extehim inded far beyond his own success. Their guidance not only helped him reach the professional stage but also shaped nto a role model for the next generation.

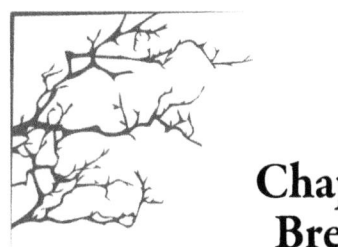

Chapter 4: First Breakthrough

Kabelo's First Trial at Farouk Khan's Academy

Kabelo Dlamini's football journey took a pivotal turn when he secured his first trial at Farouk Khan's renowned academy. Known for producing some of South Africa's most talented players, the academy was a gateway to professional football. The opportunity came unexpectedly when a scout from the academy visited Daveyton during a local tournament. Kabelo's remarkable skill on the ball and innate ability to read the game caught the scout's attention.

Kabelo's excitement was accompanied by nervous anticipation. The trial meant stepping out of the comfort of street football into a competitive, professional environment. Arriving at the academy's state-of-the-art facilities, Kabelo was awestruck. The pristine pitches, advanced equipment, and disciplined atmosphere were unlike anything he had experienced.

The trial itself was grueling. Farouk Khan's academy didn't just test physical abilities but also mental resilience and tactical awareness. Kabelo found himself among dozens of equally determined young players, all vying for a coveted spot. The drills were intense, requiring precision, speed, and focus. Despite the pressure, Kabelo's flair shone through. His quick footwork, vision, and ability to execute complex maneuvers impressed the coaches.

After days of relentless effort, Kabelo received the news he had been dreaming of—he was selected. The moment marked the beginning of his transition from a promising talent to a budding professional.

Adjusting to a Structured Football Environment and Professional Training

Joining Farouk Khan's academy was both a blessing and a challenge. For the first time, Kabelo experienced the rigor of a structured football environment. Training sessions followed a strict schedule, starting early in the morning with fitness drills, followed by technical exercises, tactical lessons, and match simulations.

The transition wasn't easy. Kabelo had to adapt to a disciplined routine that demanded physical endurance, mental sharpness, and emotional maturity. He quickly learned that talent alone wasn't enough; consistency and hard work were equally important.

One of the most significant adjustments was the emphasis on tactical awareness. In street football, instinct ruled, and creativity flowed without restriction. At the academy, Kabelo had to learn the nuances of positioning, defensive responsibilities, and strategic plays. Initially, he struggled with the structured approach, but his willingness to learn set him apart.

The academy also introduced him to a professional training regimen, including nutrition plans, strength training, and recovery techniques. Kabelo embraced these changes wholeheartedly, understanding that they were crucial for his growth. He began to see his body as an instrument that required care and maintenance to perform at its peak.

Early Signs of Talent and Determination to Succeed

From the outset, Kabelo's natural talent set him apart. Coaches marveled at his ability to maneuver through tight spaces, his impeccable first touch, and his vision for creating scoring opportunities. What stood out even more was his determination. Kabelo was often the first to arrive at training and the last to leave. He used every spare moment to improve his weaker foot, practice free kicks, or refine his dribbling. His relentless drive didn't go unnoticed. Coaches often pointed to Kabelo as an example of dedication, inspiring his peers to push themselves harder.

Off the pitch, Kabelo's humility and eagerness to learn endeared him to his teammates and coaches. He sought feedback constantly, asking questions about how he could improve and incorporating advice into his game. This willingness to grow, combined with his raw talent, made him a standout prospect.

One of the academy's most defining moments for Kabelo came during a high-stakes inter-academy match. Facing a strong opponent, Kabelo stepped up in a crucial moment, scoring two goals and assisting another. His performance cemented his reputation as a rising star and caught the attention of scouts from professional teams.

The Turning Point

Farouk Khan himself saw great potential in Kabelo. In a private conversation, he told Kabelo, "You have the talent to play at the highest level. But remember, the journey ahead is long, and success comes to those who stay focused." These words became a guiding principle for Kabelo as he progressed through the academy.

The academy didn't just hone Kabelo's skills; it instilled in him a professional mindset. He learned the importance of discipline, teamwork, and resilience—qualities that would define his career. Kabelo's time at Farouk Khan's academy was a transformative period that laid the foundation for his success, marking the beginning of a journey that would take him from the dusty streets of Daveyton to the grand stages of South African football.

This chapter in Kabelo's life was a testament to the power of hard work and the importance of seizing opportunities. While his talent opened the door, it was his determination and adaptability that solidified his place in the academy and set the stage for his ascent to greatness.

Chapter 5: The Celtic Opportunity

Kabelo's Trial at Bloemfontein Celtic

After completing his development at Farouk Khan's academy, Kabelo Dlamini's journey took another significant step forward: a trial at Bloemfontein Celtic. Known for their rich history of nurturing young talent, Celtic presented Kabelo with an opportunity to make his mark on a professional stage.

The trial was a pivotal moment in Kabelo's career. Arriving in Bloemfontein, he was met with a mix of excitement and apprehension. Kabelo was aware of Celtic's reputation for being selective, and he knew this was his chance to showcase the skills and discipline he had honed over the years.

The trial process was rigorous. Kabelo was tested on every aspect of his game—from technical ability and tactical understanding to physical fitness and mental toughness. Competing against a pool of talented players, Kabelo felt the weight of expectation. However, he thrived under the pressure. His quick decision-making, precise passing, and electrifying dribbling earned him the attention of the coaching staff.

One memorable moment during the trial was when Kabelo scored a brilliant solo goal, weaving through defenders before calmly slotting the ball into the bottom corner. This performance solidified his place, and shortly after, Kabelo received the news he had been waiting for: he had been offered a spot in Bloemfontein Celtic's MDC (MultiChoice Diski Challenge) team.

Joining the MDC Team and His Standout Performances

The MultiChoice Diski Challenge was a competitive platform designed to bridge the gap between youth development and first-team football. Joining the MDC team was a dream come true for Kabelo, but it also marked the beginning of a new set of challenges.

In the MDC, Kabelo faced some of South Africa's most promising young talents. The matches were fast-paced and physically demanding, requiring players to perform at their best consistently. Kabelo embraced the challenge, using every game as an opportunity to prove himself.

From the outset, Kabelo was a standout performer. His ability to control the tempo of the game and create goal-scoring opportunities made him a vital part of the team. Kabelo quickly became known for his composure under pressure and his knack for delivering in crucial moments.

One of his most memorable performances came in a high-stakes match against Kaizer Chiefs' MDC team. Kabelo not only scored a stunning goal but also provided two assists, leading his team to a hard-fought victory. The match earned him praise from coaches and fans alike, with many predicting a bright future for the young midfielder.

Kabelo's performances in the MDC didn't go unnoticed. The first-team coaching staff began to take an interest in his progress, and whispers of a potential promotion to the senior squad began to circulate.

Adapting to Life Away from Home

While Kabelo excelled on the pitch, his journey off the field was equally challenging. Moving to Bloemfontein meant leaving behind his family and the familiarity of Daveyton. The transition to life away from home tested Kabelo's resilience and independence.

Living in a team-provided residence with other young players, Kabelo had to adapt to a new routine. He learned to manage his own time, take care of his nutrition, and maintain a balance between football and personal life. The experience was a steep learning curve, but it also helped Kabelo grow as a person.

Loneliness and homesickness were constant companions in his early days at Celtic. Kabelo missed his family's support and the sense of community he had in Daveyton. However, he drew strength from the sacrifices they had made to help him pursue his dreams. Conversations with his family over the phone became a source of motivation, reminding him of why he had embarked on this journey.

The camaraderie within the MDC team also helped Kabelo adjust. He formed close bonds with his teammates, many of whom shared similar struggles. Together, they created a supportive environment, pushing each other to excel both on and off the field.

The Challenges of Starting Anew

Starting anew in a professional setup came with its own set of challenges. Kabelo had to earn the trust and respect of his coaches and teammates. Every training session was an opportunity to prove his worth, but it also came with the pressure to perform.

Adapting to the tactical demands of the MDC team required Kabelo to elevate his game. Unlike the academy, where individual skill was often prioritized, the MDC emphasized teamwork, discipline, and tactical execution. Kabelo worked tirelessly to align his style of play with the team's philosophy, studying game footage and seeking feedback from his coaches.

Financial challenges also played a role in Kabelo's journey. As a young player in the MDC, his earnings were modest, and he had to manage his resources carefully. Despite these difficulties, Kabelo remained focused on his long-term goals, viewing the sacrifices as an investment in his future.

Emerging as a Promising Talent

Kabelo's time in the MDC team was a period of tremendous growth. He not only honed his skills but also developed the mental toughness required to succeed in professional football. By the end of his first season, Kabelo was one of the most talked-about players in the MDC, with many tipping him for a bright future in the senior team.

The Celtic opportunity marked a turning point in Kabelo's career. It was a testament to his talent, hard work, and determination to succeed. More importantly, it was a step closer to realizing his dream of becoming a professional footballer and making his mark on South African football.

Chapter 6: Promotion to the First Team

Kabelo's Transition from MDC to the Celtic Senior Team

Kabelo Dlamini's consistent performances in the MultiChoice Diski Challenge (MDC) earned him recognition and an opportunity to step into the professional league. When the announcement came that Kabelo would be promoted to Bloemfontein Celtic's senior team, it marked a monumental moment in his journey.

The transition, however, was far from easy. Joining the senior team meant Kabelo would be competing against seasoned professionals—players with years of experience in the Premier Soccer League (PSL). The pace, physicality, and tactical demands of top-flight football were a significant step up from the MDC. Kabelo knew he had to adapt quickly to survive and thrive.

Pre-season training with the senior squad was Kabelo's first real taste of professional football at the highest level. The intensity was unlike anything he had experienced before. Every drill, every scrimmage, and every match simulation was an opportunity to prove himself. Kabelo embraced the challenge, showing the same determination and work ethic that had brought him this far.

Working Under Coach Veselin Jelusic

One of the most significant influences on Kabelo's early senior career was Coach Veselin Jelusic. Known for his emphasis on discipline, structure, and player development, Jelusic took Kabelo under his wing and played a crucial role in his transition to professional football. Jelusic recognized Kabelo's potential early on and worked closely with him to refine his skills and adapt his game to the demands of the PSL. The coach's tactical acumen and patient approach provided Kabelo with a solid foundation.

During training sessions, Jelusic often pulled Kabelo aside to offer guidance and constructive criticism. He emphasized the importance of positional awareness, decision-making, and off-the-ball movement. Under Jelusic's mentorship, Kabelo began to understand the intricacies of professional football, such as reading the game and anticipating opponents' moves.

One defining moment came during a training session when Kabelo struggled to keep up with the team's tactical drills. Instead of reprimanding him, Jelusic encouraged Kabelo to focus on his strengths and use them to complement the team's strategy. This advice boosted Kabelo's confidence and reinforced his belief in his abilities.

Learning to Thrive in the Professional League

As the PSL season approached, Kabelo's excitement was tinged with nervousness. The reality of competing against South Africa's top footballers was daunting, but Kabelo remained determined to make an impact.

His debut came in a league match against Polokwane City. Kabelo started on the bench, but as the game progressed, the coach called his name. Stepping onto the field for the first time in a professional league match, Kabelo felt a mix of adrenaline and nerves.

Although his minutes on the pitch were limited, Kabelo made an immediate impression with his composure and technical ability. He completed several key passes, created a scoring opportunity, and earned applause from both his teammates and the coaching staff.

Over the next few matches, Kabelo's role in the team grew. He was primarily utilized as an impact substitute, coming off the bench to inject energy and creativity into the team's attack. Kabelo embraced this role, using every appearance to prove his worth and learn from his more experienced teammates.

His First Professional Goals

Kabelo's first professional goal came in a league match against Baroka FC. Late in the game, Kabelo received the ball just outside the penalty area. With a quick touch to control it, he unleashed a powerful strike that soared past the goalkeeper and into the top corner of the net.

The stadium erupted in celebration, and Kabelo was mobbed by his teammates. Scoring his first goal was a milestone moment that boosted his confidence and solidified his place in the team. Kabelo described the feeling as surreal, a culmination of years of hard work and sacrifice.

His second goal came just a few weeks later in a match against AmaZulu FC. This time, Kabelo showcased his creativity and flair, dribbling past two defenders before calmly slotting the ball into the bottom corner. The goal highlighted Kabelo's technical skill and composure under pressure, earning him praise from fans and pundits alike.

Recognition from Fans

As Kabelo's performances improved, so did his popularity among Bloemfontein Celtic fans. Supporters admired his work ethic, humility, and ability to deliver in crucial moments. Kabelo quickly became a fan favorite, with many drawing comparisons to some of Celtic's all-time greats.

Fans often chanted his name during matches, and Kabelo began to feel the weight of their expectations. Rather than being overwhelmed, he used their support as motivation to push himself even harder. Kabelo made a point to engage with fans whenever possible, signing autographs and taking photos after matches.

The recognition also extended beyond Celtic's fanbase. Kabelo's performances caught the attention of football analysts and scouts, with many predicting a bright future for the young midfielder. Kabelo, however, remained grounded, focusing on improving his game and contributing to the team's success.

Balancing New Challenges

While Kabelo was enjoying his success on the field, he also faced new challenges off it. The demands of professional football required him to manage his time carefully, ensuring he maintained peak physical and mental condition. Kabelo also had to navigate the pressures of media attention and increased public scrutiny.

Through it all, Kabelo remained focused on his long-term goals. He continued to work closely with his coaches and teammates, drawing inspiration from their experiences and learning from their advice. Kabelo also maintained regular contact with his family, whose unwavering support kept him grounded and motivated.

Looking Ahead

Promotion to the first team was a defining moment in Kabelo's career. It was a testament to his talent, perseverance, and the support system that had guided him along the way. However, Kabelo knew this was only the beginning.

With every match, Kabelo grew more confident and more determined to make his mark on South African football. He dreamed of achieving even greater success—not just for himself, but for his family, his community, and the next generation of young players who looked up to him.

The transition from MDC to the Celtic senior team was Kabelo's first real taste of professional football, and it left him hungry for more. He was ready to embrace the challenges and opportunities that lay ahead, confident in his ability to rise to the occasion.

Chapter 7: Hard Work Pays Off

Building His Reputation as a Reliable Midfielder

Kabelo Dlamini's journey in the professional league was defined by his relentless work ethic and ability to adapt to challenges. As his role at Bloemfontein Celtic expanded, Kabelo began to build a reputation as a reliable and versatile midfielder.

Coaches and teammates praised Kabelo's tactical intelligence and technical ability. Whether it was breaking up opposition attacks, orchestrating plays from midfield, or creating scoring opportunities, Kabelo demonstrated a level of maturity beyond his years. His consistent performances earned him the trust of the coaching staff and made him an indispensable part of the team.

One of Kabelo's standout qualities was his ability to read the game. He had an innate sense of positioning, which allowed him to intercept passes and disrupt opponents' rhythm. Kabelo's vision and decision-making also stood out, enabling him to execute precise passes and unlock defenses with ease.

Beyond his technical skills, Kabelo's work rate set him apart. He was always willing to put in the extra effort, whether it meant tracking back to defend or making late runs into the box. Kabelo's determination and willingness to learn made him a role model for younger players in the team.

Balancing Expectations from Fans, Teammates, and Management

As Kabelo's profile grew, so did the expectations from various stakeholders. Fans expected him to deliver match-winning performances, teammates relied on him to contribute to the team's success, and management saw him as a valuable asset with potential for even greater achievements.

Balancing these expectations was not easy. Kabelo often found himself under immense pressure to perform consistently. However, he viewed this pressure as an opportunity to prove himself and demonstrate his resilience.

To manage expectations, Kabelo developed a routine that emphasized preparation and self-discipline. He dedicated time to studying opponents, analyzing his own performances, and working on areas of improvement. Kabelo also sought advice from senior teammates and mentors, who helped him navigate the demands of professional football.

Off the field, Kabelo maintained a humble and approachable demeanor. He understood the importance of connecting with fans and embraced his role as a representative of the club. Whether it was signing autographs, attending community events, or engaging with supporters on social media, Kabelo made a conscious effort to give back to those who supported him.

Overcoming Injuries and Staying Focused

Like many athletes, Kabelo faced setbacks in the form of injuries. One of the most challenging periods in his career came when he suffered a ligament strain during a training session. The injury sidelined him for several weeks, forcing him to watch from the sidelines as his team continued to compete.

For Kabelo, the recovery process was both physically and mentally demanding. He had to undergo intense physiotherapy sessions and adhere to a strict rehabilitation program. The frustration of being unable to contribute on the field tested Kabelo's patience, but he remained focused on his long-term goals.

During his recovery, Kabelo used the time to work on his mental strength. He attended team meetings, studied game footage, and visualized his return to the pitch. Kabelo's positive attitude and determination to come back stronger earned him the admiration of his teammates and coaching staff.

When Kabelo finally returned to action, he wasted no time in making an impact. In his first match back, he delivered a commanding performance, earning praise from fans and pundits alike. The experience of overcoming injury taught Kabelo valuable lessons about resilience and the importance of maintaining a strong mindset.

Recognizing the Power of Hard Work

Kabelo's journey was a testament to the power of hard work and perseverance. Every challenge he faced, whether it was proving himself on the field, meeting expectations, or overcoming setbacks, strengthened his resolve to succeed.

As Kabelo's career progressed, he continued to set ambitious goals for himself. He aspired to become one of the best midfielders in South African football and dreamed of representing his country on the international stage. Kabelo knew that achieving these goals would require unwavering dedication, but he was ready to put in the effort.

Looking Ahead

Kabelo's rise in professional football was marked by moments of triumph and adversity. Through it all, he remained grounded, drawing strength from his roots and the support of those around him. Kabelo's journey was far from over, and he was determined to make the most of every opportunity that came his way.

For Kabelo, hard work was not just a means to an end—it was a way of life. He understood that success was earned through discipline, sacrifice, and a relentless commitment to improvement. As he continued to build his legacy, Kabelo's story served as an inspiration to aspiring footballers and a reminder that greatness is achieved through perseverance.

Chapter 8: The Call from Orlando Pirates

How Kabelo Caught the Attention of One of South Africa's Biggest Clubs

By the time Kabelo Dlamini had established himself at Bloemfontein Celtic, his performances had become impossible to ignore. Week after week, his technical skills, composure under pressure, and creative play earned him accolades. Kabelo was quickly becoming one of the most exciting prospects in the league, and word of his talent began spreading beyond the Free State.

Scouts from several top clubs started attending Celtic matches, intrigued by the young midfielder's potential. Kabelo's ability to control the tempo of the game, deliver accurate set-pieces, and provide game-changing moments caught the attention of talent spotters from Orlando Pirates, one of South Africa's most storied football clubs.

What truly set Kabelo apart was his consistency. Despite playing for a mid-table team, Kabelo had proven his ability to compete at a high level against some of the PSL's toughest opponents. His standout performances against big clubs, including Pirates themselves, solidified his reputation as a player who could shine on any stage.

The buzz around Kabelo intensified during the offseason. Rumors of a potential transfer began circulating, with Orlando Pirates emerging as the frontrunners to secure his signature. For Kabelo, the idea of joining a club of Pirates' stature was both thrilling and daunting.

It represented a chance to compete for trophies, play in continental competitions, and cement his place among South Africa's football elite.

The Transfer Negotiations

The negotiations between Bloemfontein Celtic and Orlando Pirates were a closely watched affair. Celtic recognized Kabelo's value and were keen to secure a favorable deal for one of their star players. Pirates, on the other hand, saw Kabelo as a long-term investment who could strengthen their midfield and add depth to the squad.

For Kabelo, the process was filled with excitement and uncertainty. While he was eager to take the next step in his career, leaving Celtic also meant saying goodbye to the club that had given him his first professional opportunity. Kabelo remained in constant communication with his agent and mentors, seeking advice on how to navigate this critical moment in his career.

After weeks of negotiations, the deal was finalized. Kabelo Dlamini officially signed with Orlando Pirates, marking the beginning of a new chapter in his football journey. The announcement was met with widespread excitement from Pirates fans, who were eager to see what the talented midfielder would bring to their team.

Preparing for a New Chapter

Joining Orlando Pirates was a dream come true for Kabelo, but it also came with new challenges. As one of South Africa's most successful and high-profile clubs, Pirates had a rich history and a passionate fan base with high expectations. Kabelo knew that he would need to adapt quickly to the demands of playing for a team that was constantly under the spotlight.

The first step in Kabelo's transition was getting to know his new teammates and coaching staff. Pirates boasted a squad filled with experienced players and rising stars, many of whom Kabelo had admired from afar. The opportunity to train and compete alongside such talent was both inspiring and intimidating.

Preseason training with Pirates was intense. Kabelo was introduced to the club's playing philosophy, which emphasized speed, precision, and attacking football. The coaching staff worked closely with Kabelo to integrate him into the team's system, highlighting areas where he could contribute and grow.

Off the field, Kabelo faced the challenge of adjusting to life in Johannesburg. Moving from Bloemfontein to one of South Africa's busiest cities was a significant change, but Kabelo approached it with the same determination that had defined his career. He focused on staying grounded and maintaining the routines that had helped him succeed thus far.

Embracing the Buccaneers' Spirit

Kabelo's arrival at Orlando Pirates was met with a warm reception from fans and teammates alike. Known for their passionate support, Pirates fans quickly embraced Kabelo as one of their own. The nickname "Shuffle" took on new significance, symbolizing Kabelo's flair and creativity, which aligned perfectly with the club's dynamic style of play.

As Kabelo prepared for his debut, he reflected on the journey that had brought him to this point. From playing barefoot in the streets of Daveyton to signing with one of South Africa's biggest football clubs, Kabelo's story was a testament to the power of hard work, perseverance, and belief in oneself.

The call from Orlando Pirates marked the beginning of a new era for Kabelo Dlamini. It was an opportunity to showcase his talent on a larger stage, contribute to the club's legacy, and inspire the next generation of footballers. For Kabelo, this was not just the culmination of his dreams—it was the start of something even greater.

Chapter 9: Making His Mark at Pirates

Kabelo's Debut and Initial Challenges

The day of Kabelo Dlamini's Orlando Pirates debut was one he would never forget. Stepping onto the pitch wearing the iconic black-and-white jersey, Kabelo felt a mix of pride, excitement, and nervous energy. The roaring chants of the Buccaneers faithful filled the stadium, a reminder of the responsibility that came with representing one of South Africa's most storied clubs.

Despite his confidence in his abilities, adapting to Pirates' fast-paced style of play was no small feat. The team's dynamic demanded quick decision-making, precise passing, and an ability to read the game under pressure. Kabelo's first few matches were challenging, as he worked to find his rhythm and establish himself within a squad filled with seasoned professionals.

Adding to the pressure was the weight of expectations from fans and media. As a high-profile signing, Kabelo's every move was scrutinized, and he faced criticism when his performances didn't immediately meet the lofty standards associated with the club. However, Kabelo remained focused, determined to prove that he belonged at this level.

Support from Teammates

One of the key factors in Kabelo's adjustment period was the support he received from his teammates. Senior players like Happy Jele and Thembinkosi Lorch took Kabelo under their wing, offering advice and encouragement both on and off the pitch. They emphasized the importance of patience, reminding him that success at a club like Pirates required time and perseverance.

Training sessions became an opportunity for Kabelo to learn from some of the best players in the league. He observed their techniques, studied their movements, and sought feedback on how he could improve his own game. This collaborative environment fostered a sense of camaraderie that helped Kabelo feel more at home within the team.

Lessons from Coach Micho

Under the guidance of Coach Milutin "Micho" Sredojević, Kabelo began to understand the nuances of Pirates' tactical approach. Micho, known for his meticulous attention to detail, worked closely with Kabelo to refine his skills and integrate him into the team's strategy.

Micho encouraged Kabelo to play to his strengths—his creativity, vision, and ability to control the tempo of the game. At the same time, he challenged Kabelo to improve in areas such as defensive positioning and off-the-ball movement. These lessons proved invaluable, as they helped Kabelo become a more well-rounded player.

One pivotal moment in Kabelo's development came during a post-match review session with Micho. After a particularly challenging game, the coach highlighted both Kabelo's mistakes and his moments of brilliance. Instead of dwelling on the negatives, Micho used the session as an opportunity to build Kabelo's confidence, emphasizing his potential to become a key player for the team.

Finding His Place

As the season progressed, Kabelo began to find his footing. His growing confidence was evident in his performances, as he started contributing to the team with crucial assists, precise passes, and even a few memorable goals. Fans began to take notice of Kabelo's talent, and the nickname "Shuffle" became synonymous with his ability to dazzle opponents with his skillful play.

Kabelo's turning point came during a high-stakes match against one of Pirates' biggest rivals. With the game tied and tensions running high, Kabelo delivered a game-winning assist that showcased his vision and composure under pressure. The moment was a testament to his growth and resilience, proving that he was capable of thriving on the biggest stages.

The Start of Something Special

By the end of his first season with Orlando Pirates, Kabelo had firmly established himself as a valuable member of the squad. While the journey had not been without its challenges, Kabelo's determination, hard work, and willingness to learn had earned him the respect of his teammates, coaches, and fans.

For Kabelo, the experience of making his mark at Pirates was a reminder of the importance of perseverance and self-belief. It was also a stepping stone toward achieving even greater heights in his career. With his debut season behind him, Kabelo was ready to embrace the challenges and opportunities that lay ahead as a Buccaneer.

Chapter 10: The Zinnbauer Era

His Enhanced Role Under Coach Josef Zinnbauer

The arrival of Coach Josef Zinnbauer at Orlando Pirates marked a turning point in Kabelo Dlamini's career. Known for his tactical acumen and emphasis on teamwork, Zinnbauer immediately identified Kabelo as a player with untapped potential. The coach's vision for the team emphasized creativity and fluidity in the midfield, qualities that aligned perfectly with Kabelo's style of play.

Under Zinnbauer's leadership, Kabelo was given an enhanced role in the squad. He became a pivotal figure in the team's build-up play, tasked with linking defense and attack through his precise passing and vision. Zinnbauer also encouraged Kabelo to take on more responsibility in high-pressure situations, challenging him to step out of his comfort zone and become a leader on the pitch.

One of Zinnbauer's most significant contributions to Kabelo's development was his ability to instill confidence. During one-on-one meetings, the coach praised Kabelo's technical skills while providing constructive feedback on areas for improvement. These sessions helped Kabelo refine his game, and he began to flourish in his new role.

Handling Criticism and Using It as Motivation

Despite his growing importance to the team, Kabelo wasn't immune to criticism. Fans and pundits often scrutinized his performances, with some questioning his consistency and ability to deliver in crucial matches. Kabelo, however, viewed criticism as an opportunity for growth.

Rather than letting negative comments affect his morale, Kabelo used them as fuel to prove his doubters wrong. He spent extra hours on the training ground, working tirelessly to improve his fitness, technique, and decision-making. This dedication paid off, as Kabelo's performances began to speak for themselves.

A defining moment came during a post-match interview, where Kabelo was asked about the pressures of playing for a club like Pirates. His response was a testament to his resilience: "Criticism is part of the game. It pushes me to be better, to work harder, and to show everyone why I deserve to wear this jersey."

Playing Alongside Top Talents

The Zinnbauer era saw Kabelo playing alongside some of the best talents in South African football. Sharing the pitch with players like Thembinkosi Lorch, Vincent Pule, and Deon Hotto not only elevated Kabelo's game but also deepened his understanding of teamwork and chemistry.

These collaborations led to some memorable moments on the pitch. Kabelo's ability to read the game and deliver precise passes made him an invaluable asset to the team's attacking play. His partnership with Lorch, in particular, became a highlight for fans, as the duo combined to create numerous goal-scoring opportunities.

Off the pitch, Kabelo built strong relationships with his teammates, learning from their experiences and drawing inspiration from their success stories. The camaraderie within the squad created a positive atmosphere that translated into improved performances on match days.

Becoming a Fan Favorite

As Kabelo's influence on the team grew, so did his popularity among the Buccaneers' faithful. Fans admired his work ethic, humility, and unwavering commitment to the club. Kabelo's performances often left the crowd in awe, with his flair and creativity earning him standing ovations and chants of "Shuffle!" during matches.

Beyond his contributions on the field, Kabelo also made an effort to connect with the community. He participated in outreach programs, youth football clinics, and fan meet-and-greet events, further endearing himself to the Pirates' supporters. For Kabelo, these interactions were a way to give back to the fans who had supported him through thick and thin.

A Season to Remember

By the end of the season, Kabelo had cemented his place as one of Orlando Pirates' most reliable and exciting players. His journey under Coach Zinnbauer was a testament to his growth, both as a player and as an individual. Kabelo's enhanced role, combined with his ability to overcome challenges, had solidified his status as a key figure in the team's success.

Looking back on the Zinnbauer era, Kabelo recognized it as a transformative period in his career. It was a time of learning, growth, and self-discovery—a chapter that prepared him for the challenges and opportunities that lay ahead.

Chapter 11: Pursuing National Dreams

A Childhood Dream

From the bustling streets of Daveyton to the grand stadiums of the Premier Soccer League (PSL), Kabelo Dlamini has always carried one dream close to his heart: representing South Africa as part of Bafana Bafana. For Kabelo, wearing the national team jersey is more than just an ambition—it is the ultimate validation of his talent, dedication, and sacrifices.

Growing up, Kabelo would gather with his friends and family to watch South Africa's national team take on Africa's and the world's best. He vividly remembers the electrifying atmosphere during the 2010 FIFA World Cup, hosted on home soil. Even though Bafana Bafana didn't progress far, the pride of seeing South Africa on the global stage inspired him. From that moment on, Kabelo set his sights on one day being part of the team that would rewrite the country's football legacy.

The Road to Recognition

As Kabelo climbed the ranks in South African football, his dream of playing for the national team remained a guiding force. Every game for Orlando Pirates was an opportunity to showcase his skills and catch the eye of the national selectors.

He was aware of the challenges. South Africa boasts a wealth of footballing talent, and the competition for places in the national squad is fierce. Kabelo also understood that consistency in club football is key to earning a call-up. For him, every moment on the pitch mattered—each pass, dribble, and goal brought him closer to being noticed.

Learning from National Heroes

Even without a call-up, Kabelo has drawn inspiration from the journeys of other Bafana Bafana players. He admires legends like Teko Modise, a midfield maestro who overcame personal and professional challenges to become one of South Africa's most celebrated players. Kabelo often reflects on how players like Modise made the leap from local leagues to the international stage.

Kabelo is also inspired by current stars like Themba Zwane, whose creativity and composure on the ball have earned him accolades both domestically and internationally. Watching Zwane's success reminds Kabelo that hard work and perseverance can pave the way to a Bafana Bafana debut.

A Journey of Growth

While Kabelo hasn't yet received the call to represent his country, he views this as part of his growth as a player. He understands that timing is everything, and he's committed to staying prepared for when his opportunity comes.

Kabelo has set personal goals to enhance his chances of national team selection. These include improving his versatility as a player, mastering multiple roles in midfield, and developing the consistency that national selectors value. Kabelo spends countless hours studying his own game and seeking feedback from coaches and teammates.

Off the pitch, Kabelo's discipline and professionalism are evident. He maintains a rigorous fitness regimen, works closely with Orlando

Pirates' technical staff, and remains focused on his long-term ambitions. His humility and willingness to learn have earned him respect within the football community, further solidifying his reputation as a future prospect for Bafana Bafana.

Support from Fans and Teammates

One of Kabelo's biggest motivators is the unwavering support he receives from fans, especially those in Daveyton. Many in his hometown see him as a beacon of hope and believe it's only a matter of time before he gets his chance on the international stage.

His Orlando Pirates teammates also encourage him. They often remind Kabelo of his potential and share their own experiences of representing South Africa. Hearing stories from players who have donned the green and gold motivates Kabelo to keep pushing himself.

Looking to the Future

Kabelo remains optimistic about his chances of one day joining Bafana Bafana. He envisions himself playing at the Africa Cup of Nations, representing South Africa in World Cup qualifiers, and helping the team reclaim its place as one of Africa's footballing powerhouses.

For Kabelo, the journey to the national team is not just about personal achievement. It's about inspiring the next generation of players in Daveyton and across South Africa. He wants to show young footballers that dreams are achievable with hard work and perseverance.

While the call-up remains a dream, Kabelo's journey is far from over. He continues to work tirelessly, knowing that his opportunity could come at any moment. Until then, he will keep giving his all for Orlando Pirates, honing his skills, and preparing for the day when he can proudly represent South Africa on the international stage.

Chapter 12: Champions League Aspirations

The Dream of African Glory

For Kabelo Dlamini, stepping onto the field during a CAF Champions League match isn't just about representing Orlando Pirates; it's about showcasing South African football on the grandest stage of the continent. From the time he started playing football in the streets of Daveyton, Kabelo has dreamt of testing his skills against Africa's finest.

The CAF Champions League is a tournament that carries immense prestige. For Kabelo, it represents the culmination of years of hard work and the realization of his potential as a professional footballer. The thought of competing in iconic stadiums like Cairo International Stadium in Egypt or Stade Mohamed V in Morocco motivates him to push harder every day.

The Weight of History

Orlando Pirates' history in the CAF Champions League adds a sense of responsibility to Kabelo's aspirations. The club's 1995 triumph remains one of the proudest moments in South African football history, a benchmark that Kabelo and his teammates aim to replicate.

Growing up, Kabelo heard stories of the 1995 team's resilience, unity, and tactical brilliance. Players like Edward Motale and Jerry Sikhosana became legends not only for their performances on the pitch but for their role in putting South African football on the map.

Kabelo's determination to emulate their success is evident in how he approaches training and matches.

"Playing for a club with such a legacy is an honor," Kabelo often reflects. "It reminds me that we're not just playing for ourselves but for everyone who loves the badge."

Early Setbacks in Continental Campaigns

Despite Orlando Pirates' rich history, Kabelo has experienced the harsh realities of competing at the continental level. One of the toughest moments in his career was the team's failure to progress past the group stages in a recent CAF Champions League campaign.

Kabelo recalls the crushing disappointment of those early exits, not just for the team but for the passionate fans who had high hopes. The losses taught him valuable lessons about the importance of preparation, mental fortitude, and consistency in a competition where the stakes are always high.

"These moments were tough, but they were also necessary," Kabelo says. "They made us realize what it takes to compete at the highest level. You can't take anything for granted in the Champions League."

Adapting to Continental Football

One of the most significant challenges Kabelo has faced in continental competitions is adapting to the diverse styles of play. African football is a melting pot of different approaches, from the highly tactical and disciplined North African teams to the physically demanding and fast-paced West African sides.

Kabelo speaks about how these experiences have shaped him as a player. "In the Champions League, every game feels like a final. You're playing against teams that are champions in their countries, and they bring their best. It's taught me to be smarter, quicker, and more adaptable."

The grueling travel schedules, unfamiliar conditions, and hostile crowds add another layer of complexity. Kabelo vividly remembers playing in a packed stadium in Kinshasa, where the fans' energy created an atmosphere unlike anything he had experienced before. These challenges, however, have only strengthened his resolve to succeed.

Personal Growth and Commitment

For Kabelo, the journey to achieving Champions League success has been as much about personal growth as it has been about football. The disappointment of early exits forced him to confront his weaknesses and work tirelessly to improve.

Kabelo has focused on several aspects of his game, including his stamina, passing accuracy, and decision-making under pressure. He spends hours analyzing footage of past Champions League games, studying the movements and strategies of top players. "Every detail matters in this competition," he says. "You have to be at your best in every moment."

His commitment extends beyond the pitch. Kabelo has also taken steps to ensure he is mentally prepared for the demands of continental football. He works with sports psychologists to build his confidence and maintain focus, even in the face of adversity.

Team Dynamics and Leadership

Kabelo understands that individual brilliance can only take a team so far in the Champions League. Success in this competition requires cohesion, trust, and leadership. Kabelo has emerged as a vocal presence in the Orlando Pirates dressing room, encouraging his teammates to give their all and believe in their abilities.

He often draws on his own experiences to motivate younger players, reminding them of the importance of resilience and hard work. "We're all in this together," he says. "If we fight for each other, there's nothing we can't achieve."

Inspiration from African Legends

Kabelo's dream of Champions League glory is fueled by the achievements of African football legends. He often cites Pitso Mosimane, whose coaching successes with Mamelodi Sundowns and Al Ahly have set a new standard for African football.

"Pitso showed us what's possible," Kabelo says. "He's a reminder that we, as Africans, can compete with the best in the world."

He also admires players like Didier Drogba and Samuel Eto'o, who dominated European competitions after starting their careers in Africa. Their stories inspire Kabelo to believe that his journey, too, can reach incredible heights.

Future Goals and Determination

Kabelo's ultimate goal is to help Orlando Pirates lift the CAF Champions League trophy once again. He envisions the day he will stand on the podium, medal around his neck, holding the trophy aloft in front of jubilant fans.

For Kabelo, this dream is about more than personal achievement. It's about giving back to the community that raised him, inspiring the next generation of players, and proving that South African football belongs on the global stage.

"Winning the Champions League would be a dream come true," he says. "But it's also a responsibility. It's about showing the world what we're capable of as a team and as a country."

As Kabelo continues his journey, he remains focused, driven, and hopeful. The road to continental glory is fraught with challenges, but Kabelo is prepared to face them head-on, determined to make his mark in African football history.

Chapter 13: Loyalty to the Buccaneers

The Power of Loyalty

In modern football, where lucrative contracts and transfer rumors dominate headlines, Kabelo Dlamini stands out as a player who values loyalty. His unwavering commitment to Orlando Pirates is not just about wearing the jersey but embracing the culture and history of the club.

Despite receiving offers from other clubs and speculation about potential moves, Kabelo has consistently chosen to stay with the Buccaneers. For him, Orlando Pirates is more than just a team—it's a family, a legacy, and a platform to achieve greatness.

"Being part of this club is an honor," Kabelo often says. "It's not just about what the club does for me, but what I can do for the club."

Navigating Transfer Rumors

At various points in his career, Kabelo has been linked with moves to rival South African teams and even clubs abroad. These rumors often create distractions for players, but Kabelo has managed to stay grounded.

"I've learned to block out the noise," he explains. "People will always talk, but I know where my heart is."

Kabelo acknowledges that opportunities to play for other teams can be tempting, especially when they come with promises of higher salaries and new challenges. However, his love for Orlando Pirates and his desire to contribute to the team's success have always outweighed these considerations.

Relationships with Teammates and Coaches

One of the reasons Kabelo feels so connected to Orlando Pirates is the bond he shares with his teammates and coaching staff. Over the years, he has developed close relationships with players who share his passion and drive.

Kabelo often mentions how senior players like Happy Jele and Thembinkosi Lorch mentored him when he first joined the team. Their guidance helped him adjust to the pressures of playing for a big club and inspired him to take on a leadership role as he gained experience.

Coaches, too, have played a significant role in Kabelo's loyalty to the club. Each coach he has worked under, from Micho to Josef Zinnbauer and now José Riveiro, has brought unique perspectives and challenges that have helped him grow as a player. Kabelo speaks highly of their influence, emphasizing that their trust in him has been a major factor in his decision to stay.

The Fans' Influence

Kabelo often cites the passionate Orlando Pirates fans as one of the main reasons for his loyalty. From the roaring chants at Orlando Stadium to the messages of support on social media, the fans have made Kabelo feel like an integral part of the club's identity.

"I play for them," Kabelo says with a smile. "Their energy, their belief—it pushes me to give my best every time I step onto the field."

He recalls moments when fans have lifted the team during challenging matches, creating an atmosphere that makes opponents feel the weight of the Buccaneers' legacy. Kabelo feels a deep responsibility to repay their faith with consistent performances and dedication.

Building a Legacy

For Kabelo, staying with Orlando Pirates is about more than loyalty—it's about building a legacy. He wants to be remembered as one of the players who helped restore the club to its former glory, winning trophies and setting an example for future generations.

"Pirates is a club with a proud history," he says. "I want to be part of the story that future players will look up to."

Kabelo's commitment to this vision is evident in how he approaches his role on and off the pitch. He takes every game seriously, knowing that each performance contributes to the club's reputation and his own legacy.

Turning Down Lucrative Offers

At one point, Kabelo received an offer from a Middle Eastern club, promising a significant salary increase and the chance to play in an international league. While many players would have jumped at the opportunity, Kabelo chose to stay with Orlando Pirates.

"It wasn't an easy decision," he admits. "But I realized that money isn't everything. What matters most is where you feel at home, where you can make the biggest impact."

Kabelo's decision earned him respect from his teammates, coaches, and fans, reinforcing his status as a loyal and dedicated Buccaneer.

Preparing for the Future

While Kabelo is fully committed to Orlando Pirates, he also recognizes the importance of preparing for the future. He has expressed interest in exploring opportunities to play abroad someday, not for financial gain but to challenge himself and represent South African football on a global stage.

"If the right opportunity comes, I'll consider it," Kabelo says. "But for now, my focus is on Pirates and helping the team achieve its goals."

In the meantime, Kabelo continues to work on his skills, knowing that staying competitive is essential in today's football world. He spends extra hours in training, studies his opponents, and stays updated on the latest trends in football tactics.

Loyalty as a Message

Kabelo hopes that his loyalty to Orlando Pirates sends a powerful message to young players. In an era where loyalty is often overshadowed by financial incentives, Kabelo wants to show that staying true to your roots and your team can be just as rewarding.

"Football isn't just a job," he says. "It's about passion, pride, and making a difference. When you play for a team like Pirates, you're not just playing for yourself—you're playing for millions of fans, for history, and for the future."

Looking Ahead

As Kabelo continues his journey with Orlando Pirates, he remains optimistic about the team's potential. He believes that with hard work, unity, and determination, the Buccaneers can achieve greatness once again.

"I see a bright future for this team," he says confidently. "And I'm proud to be part of it."

For Kabelo Dlamini, loyalty isn't just a choice—it's a way of life. And as he looks ahead to the challenges and opportunities that lie ahead, he does so with the unwavering belief that his best days with Orlando Pirates are still to come.

Chapter 14: Overcoming Adversity and Staying Focused

The Unexpected Challenges

In the world of professional football, every player faces adversity at some point. For Kabelo Dlamini, the road to success hasn't always been smooth. Throughout his career, he's encountered setbacks that could have derailed his ambitions. From injuries to moments of doubt, Kabelo has learned that overcoming adversity is a fundamental part of his journey.

One of the first significant challenges came early in his career when he suffered a series of minor injuries that prevented him from reaching his full potential. These injuries were frustrating for a young player trying to make an impact. "When you're sidelined, it's tough," Kabelo admits. "You feel like you're letting your team down, and you start to question yourself. But I always try to stay focused on the bigger picture."

Despite the physical setbacks, Kabelo didn't let them define him. Instead of giving into frustration, he used the time off to work on other aspects of his game—whether it was improving his fitness, refining his technical skills, or watching footage of top players to better understand the nuances of his position.

The Mental Struggles

While injuries posed physical challenges, the mental hurdles were just as difficult. Football, at its core, is a mental game, and Kabelo learned early on that the mental side of the sport is just as important as physical ability.

The pressure of representing a club as big as Orlando Pirates often weighed heavily on Kabelo, especially during periods of poor team performance. "When things aren't going well for the team, it's easy to get discouraged," he reflects. "But I've learned to keep pushing, even when things feel like they're falling apart."

At times, he would feel the weight of expectations—both from the fans and the club—to deliver top performances every match. He admits there were moments when self-doubt crept in. But through perseverance and mental fortitude, Kabelo learned how to handle these pressures and turn them into motivation.

"I remind myself that I'm here for a reason," he explains. "The coach trusts me, my teammates believe in me, and most importantly, I believe in myself. That's what keeps me going."

Family Support: The Foundation

During these challenging times, Kabelo always turned to his family for support. His parents, siblings, and extended family have been his pillars throughout his journey, providing him with the encouragement he needed to stay focused.

His mother, in particular, has been a constant source of strength. "She's always there, reminding me of how far I've come and how much I've sacrificed," Kabelo says. "Her belief in me is unshakable, and that's what keeps me grounded."

His family also played a crucial role in helping him manage his career outside of football. When the stress of professional football became overwhelming, Kabelo would take time off to visit his family in Daveyton, where he could recharge and reconnect with his roots.

"I've always said that family is everything," he reflects. "They remind me that football is just a part of who I am. It's what I do, not who I am."

Handling Criticism and Negative Media

As a high-profile player for one of South Africa's most beloved football clubs, Kabelo inevitably faced his fair share of criticism. The media, in particular, can be unforgiving, and Kabelo's performances often came under intense scrutiny.

There were times when headlines questioned his form, his decisions on the pitch, and even his commitment to the club. However, Kabelo learned to rise above the noise.

"It's tough to hear the criticism, especially when it's personal," he admits. "But I've learned that not all criticism is bad. Some of it helps you grow, helps you realize where you can improve. And the rest? You just have to let it slide off your back."

Kabelo credits his growth in handling criticism to his mentors and coaches, who have instilled in him the importance of resilience. "They taught me that you can't let external factors control your mind," he says. "Your focus needs to be on what you can control—your performance, your attitude, your professionalism."

Injury Setbacks and the Comeback

Perhaps the biggest test of Kabelo's perseverance came after he sustained a serious injury that sidelined him for several months. At the peak of his career, just when things were looking promising, a knee injury threatened to derail his progress.

"It was devastating," he confesses. "You work so hard to get to a certain level, and in one moment, everything changes. I was scared. I didn't know how long it would take to recover, and I feared it would be the end of my time at Pirates."

But Kabelo's commitment to returning stronger was unwavering. He underwent extensive rehabilitation, working closely with the medical team to regain full fitness. Throughout the process, he kept a positive mindset, focusing on the goal of returning to the pitch as a better player.

"It was a difficult time, but I kept telling myself that the only way out was through," Kabelo says. "The injury wasn't going to define me. I was going to come back, and when I did, I'd be even stronger."

Kabelo's journey back to the field was marked by hard work and determination. He spent hours on the training pitch, working not just on his fitness but also on his mental toughness. When he finally returned to competitive action, it was clear that the time away had not diminished his drive or his skill.

Finding Balance and Avoiding Burnout

As his career continued to flourish, Kabelo found himself juggling the pressures of being a professional footballer with the demands of daily life. He learned the importance of balancing his personal and professional life, ensuring that the intensity of football didn't take a toll on his mental and emotional well-being.

"I've learned that it's okay to take a step back sometimes," he says. "You can't give everything to football, because eventually, it takes everything from you. Finding that balance has been key for me."

Kabelo now makes time for activities outside of football that allow him to unwind. Whether it's spending time with his family, traveling, or pursuing hobbies that have nothing to do with the sport, Kabelo believes that these moments of reprieve are vital for maintaining his focus and drive when it's time to step onto the pitch.

"I don't want to burn out," Kabelo admits. "I love football, but I also know it's important to have other things that make you happy and keep you grounded."

A Stronger Mindset

Today, Kabelo is a player with a stronger, more resilient mindset. He knows how to handle adversity, both on and off the pitch. His journey has taught him that success doesn't come without obstacles, but it's how you respond to those obstacles that defines your career.

"I've faced a lot of challenges, but I've always found a way to overcome them," he says. "Football is about growth. It's about constantly improving and pushing past your limits. And that's what I aim to do every day."

For Kabelo, the ability to stay focused, even during tough times, has been crucial to his success. His journey is a testament to the power of perseverance, hard work, and maintaining a positive mindset, no matter the obstacles in front of you.

"Every setback is just another lesson," Kabelo says with a smile. "And I'm not done yet. There's still so much more to achieve."

Chapter 15: The Zinnbauer Era and Personal Growth

A New Chapter Under Coach Zinnbauer

Kabelo Dlamini's journey at Orlando Pirates took a significant turn with the arrival of Coach Josef Zinnbauer. The German tactician brought with him a fresh tactical approach and a high level of discipline that would challenge every player to elevate their game. For Kabelo, this was both an opportunity and a challenge, as he had to adapt quickly to the new system while continuing to prove his worth on the field.

"I remember the first training session with Coach Zinnbauer. The intensity was on another level. The focus on tactical discipline and quick decision-making was something I had never experienced before," Kabelo recalls. "It was tough at first, but I quickly realized that if I wanted to be part of this team, I had to buy into his philosophy."

Under Zinnbauer, Kabelo found himself developing into a more complete player. The coach's focus on technical precision and teamwork complemented Kabelo's natural abilities. He had to refine his positioning, work on his defensive contributions, and become more versatile in midfield.

"I'd always seen myself as an attacking player, but Coach Zinnbauer taught me the importance of balancing defense and attack," Kabelo explains. "In football, you have to understand the game in its entirety, not just one side of it. And that's what he made me realize."

The Tactical Demands of the New System

The tactical demands under Zinnbauer were different from what Kabelo had been accustomed to. The coach's preferred 4-2-3-1 formation required a fluid style of play, where midfielders had to constantly shift roles depending on the situation. Kabelo, known for his dribbling and technical prowess, was asked to add more depth to his game—contributing defensively when needed and also playing a more disciplined, structured role in midfield.

At first, the adjustments were difficult, especially for a player who had spent much of his career excelling in a free-flowing style. However, Kabelo's adaptability became one of his strongest assets.

"Coach Zinnbauer taught me the importance of being a complete midfielder," Kabelo says. "He wanted me to contribute on both ends of the pitch—defending, transitioning the ball, and creating chances. I had to improve my awareness and my decision-making. It was tough, but it made me a better player."

Facing Criticism and Building Mental Toughness

As Kabelo adapted to the new system, his performances were under constant scrutiny. While some fans were thrilled to see him rise to the challenge, others were critical of his adjustments, feeling that he wasn't quite the same player they had seen in previous seasons.

It was during these moments of criticism that Kabelo's mental toughness was tested. He had to confront the reality that not everyone would be satisfied with his performance all the time. The criticism stung, but it also fueled his determination to improve.

"Being a professional footballer means dealing with criticism," Kabelo admits. "It's tough, especially when it feels personal. But I've learned to use that criticism as motivation. I know I'm capable of more, and every time someone doubts me, it just pushes me to work harder."

Kabelo credits his growth during this period to the support of his teammates and the coaching staff. While the pressure from fans and the media was intense, his teammates were always there to remind him of his value.

"We all went through it together," Kabelo says. "Coach Zinnbauer is very supportive, and my teammates made sure I stayed focused. We knew the goal was to improve as a team, and that meant helping each other through tough times."

Embracing Leadership Responsibilities

As Kabelo's role in the team grew, he began to take on more leadership responsibilities. While he wasn't yet an official captain, he became one of the key voices in the dressing room. His experience, combined with his natural leadership qualities, made him a player that younger teammates looked up to for guidance.

"I never saw myself as a leader at first, but as I grew, I realized the importance of being vocal and leading by example," Kabelo says. "It's not always about what you say; it's about how you carry yourself. You have to show the younger players what it means to be a professional."

His leadership was evident both on and off the pitch. Kabelo took time to mentor some of the younger players, sharing the lessons he had learned over the years. He often found himself in one-on-one conversations with rising stars, offering advice on handling the pressures of playing for a big club like Pirates.

"It's all about keeping your head level," Kabelo explains. "When you're young and just starting out, it can be overwhelming. But you have to remember that the pressure is part of the game. It's how you respond to it that matters."

The Challenges of Balancing Expectations

Under Zinnbauer, the expectations at Orlando Pirates were higher than ever. The team's performance in domestic competitions, especially the league, was a constant topic of discussion. Fans expected nothing less than success, and every dropped point was scrutinized. Kabelo, as a senior member of the squad, felt the weight of these expectations acutely.

"There's always pressure to win at a club like Pirates," Kabelo says. "The fans are passionate, and they expect us to be at our best every single match. It's a big responsibility, but it's also a privilege to represent a club with such rich history."

Despite the pressure, Kabelo found ways to manage expectations. His focus remained on improving as a player and helping the team achieve its goals, rather than getting distracted by the constant noise.

"I've learned that you can't control what others expect from you," he says. "What you can control is your performance. If I give my best every game, I know I've done my part. That's the mentality I try to bring to every match."

Playing Alongside Top Talents

One of the most rewarding aspects of Kabelo's time under Zinnbauer was the opportunity to play alongside some of the best talent in South African football. The Pirates squad was filled with experienced players, each with their own unique style and abilities. Playing alongside them gave Kabelo the chance to learn from some of the best in the business.

"I've had the privilege of playing with some incredible players at Pirates," Kabelo says. "Guys like Thembinkosi Lorch, Happy Jele, and Richard Ofori are amazing professionals, and I've learned so much from them. You see how they approach the game, how disciplined they are, and it inspires you to push harder."

One of the standout players Kabelo mentions is his midfield partner, Ben Motshwari. "Ben is a player I really look up to. We have a great partnership in midfield, and we push each other to be better. It's that kind of competition that helps elevate everyone's game."

Playing alongside such talent has not only improved Kabelo's game but also given him the confidence to thrive in high-pressure situations. Whether it's a crucial league match or a cup final, Kabelo knows that he's not alone.

The Evolution of Kabelo Dlamini

As his career progressed, Kabelo Dlamini's evolution as a player was evident in every aspect of his game. He was no longer just the energetic, flair-driven player who had joined Pirates years ago. Under Zinnbauer, Kabelo became a more complete and balanced midfielder—one who could dominate both sides of the pitch.

"I've definitely evolved as a player," Kabelo reflects. "Coach Zinnbauer's influence has been huge in that. He's helped me become more tactical, more aware of the game as a whole. I'm not just focusing on what I can do with the ball; I'm also focusing on how I can help the team defensively, how I can dictate play, and how I can read the game better."

Today, Kabelo is one of the most well-rounded and dependable players in the Pirates squad, a player who can be counted on in both attacking and defensive situations.

"I'm proud of how far I've come," Kabelo says. "But I know there's always room to grow. Every day, I'm working to become the best version of myself—on the pitch and off it."

As his career continues to flourish under Coach Zinnbauer, Kabelo Dlamini's story is a testament to the power of self-belief, adaptability, and a relentless work ethic.

Chapter 16: The Road to Continental Glory

The Dream of Continental Success

As Kabelo Dlamini's career continued to soar at Orlando Pirates, one goal remained firmly entrenched in his mind: to achieve continental glory. For any player at a club like Pirates, competing in the CAF Champions League is one of the ultimate aspirations. The competition is filled with some of Africa's finest teams, and its prestige is a badge of honor for those who succeed. Kabelo, having already experienced significant success domestically, now set his sights on winning Africa's premier club competition.

"The Champions League is something every African footballer dreams of," Kabelo says. "It's the ultimate test. If you can perform in that competition, you know you're among the best in Africa. For a club like Pirates, it's the goal. We want to bring that trophy back to South Africa."

His ambition was shared by his teammates, the technical staff, and the entire Orlando Pirates faithful. The team had a rich history in the tournament, with the 1995 victory etched in the annals of South African football. However, more than two decades later, the club had yet to win a second continental title, and Kabelo was determined to play his part in ending that drought.

The Build-Up to Continental Campaigns

In the build-up to their Champions League campaign, Pirates had a team that was brimming with potential. The squad had improved significantly under the guidance of Coach Zinnbauer, and with players like Kabelo leading from the front, expectations for success on the continental stage were higher than ever. The team had qualified for the Champions League by virtue of their success in the domestic league, and with the addition of key signings, there was an overwhelming sense of optimism.

"The feeling in the camp was one of excitement," Kabelo recalls. "We knew the road ahead wouldn't be easy, but we were ready for it. We had a squad full of talent, and we believed that we could compete with anyone in Africa. Our goal was simple—win the Champions League."

Kabelo was a central figure in the team, his creativity and technical ability crucial for orchestrating the Pirates' attack. His partnership with midfielders like Ben Motshwari and the defensive stability provided by players like Happy Jele and Thulani Hlatshwayo gave Pirates the perfect mix of balance and flair. The team, more than ever, was ready to challenge the best Africa had to offer.

The Intensity of CAF Champions League Football

The Champions League group stages presented the first major challenge for Pirates. Their opponents were no strangers to African football's elite—teams that had been dominant in their respective leagues and were looking to add continental glory to their histories. Each game was a test of skill, endurance, and character. The intensity of CAF football was something Kabelo quickly recognized as different from what he had faced in domestic competitions.

"The level of competition in the Champions League is just on another level," Kabelo says. "The teams are tactically solid, and the physicality is unmatched. It's a different kind of football. Every match feels like a final, and the atmosphere in those stadiums is electric. You can't afford to make mistakes. One mistake could end your campaign."

The pressure was intense, but it also brought out the best in Kabelo. His ability to control the midfield, win possession, and distribute the ball effectively was crucial to Pirates' campaign. He thrived in the fast-paced, high-pressure environment of continental football.

However, the challenges were real. As Pirates faced some of the continent's strongest sides, they quickly realized that the road to the final was going to be long and difficult. Every game required maximum effort, and no lead was ever secure. Despite the fierce competition, Kabelo and his teammates remained focused, determined to see the journey through.

Setbacks and Resilience

While Pirates managed to perform admirably during the group stages, the road to the knockout rounds was not without its challenges. Early in their campaign, the team experienced setbacks, including a tough loss at home to one of their continental rivals. For a club with such a rich history, home defeats in international competitions were difficult to accept.

"We had to take a hard look at ourselves after that loss," Kabelo says. "It was painful, but we knew that if we wanted to make it to the final, we had to dig deep. We couldn't let that setback derail us. We had to show resilience."

The defeat served as a wake-up call, motivating Pirates to tighten their defense and become more clinical in front of goal. Kabelo's leadership on the pitch helped the team refocus, and they came back stronger in the following games. Their collective resilience paid off as they qualified for the knockout stages, setting up a thrilling campaign to reach the final.

"Every match from that point was a cup final," Kabelo reflects. "We knew that to win the Champions League, we had to keep improving with each game. We didn't take anything for granted. The focus was on winning, no matter the opponent."

The Road to the Final

The knockout stages of the CAF Champions League saw Pirates go head-to-head with some of Africa's top clubs. Their path to the final was filled with dramatic moments—last-minute goals, thrilling comebacks, and breathtaking performances from Kabelo and his teammates.

"The Champions League is unpredictable," Kabelo says. "One moment you're celebrating, and the next, you're trying to regroup after conceding a goal. The key is to stay calm and keep believing in yourself and your team. We always knew that if we played our best football, we could make it to the final."

For Kabelo, this was the culmination of years of hard work. He was living his dream, playing in the biggest club competition in African football. As the team advanced through the rounds, the pressure mounted, but so did the desire to win. Pirates' fans rallied behind the team, filling stadiums with chants and songs of support.

"I've never experienced anything like the atmosphere in those Champions League matches," Kabelo says. "The energy from the fans is unbelievable. They believe in us, and that belief fuels us. We can't let them down."

The Final Push

As the final approached, the excitement reached fever pitch. Pirates' opponents in the final were one of the strongest clubs in Africa, and the challenge was daunting. But Kabelo, along with his teammates, was determined to give everything for the chance to lift the Champions League trophy.

"We knew that the final would be the toughest match of our lives," Kabelo says. "But we also knew that we had the talent and the belief to win. We had to make it count. The players, the coaches, and the fans all believed that this was our time."

Despite giving their all in the final, Orlando Pirates fell short, missing out on the coveted Champions League trophy. The defeat was a heartbreaking one for Kabelo and his teammates, but it also served as a powerful reminder of just how close they had come to achieving continental glory.

Looking to the Future

Though they didn't win the Champions League that year, Kabelo's journey through the competition had a lasting impact. The experience of playing at such a high level, the lessons learned from the setbacks, and the bond forged with his teammates became key pillars of his career. He understood that while the road to continental glory was difficult, it was also one worth traveling.

"We're not giving up," Kabelo says with resolve. "We've come so far, and we'll be back stronger. This loss hurts, but it fuels our hunger for the future. The next time we're in the final, we'll be ready to win. This is just the beginning for us."

Kabelo Dlamini's journey in the CAF Champions League may not have ended with a trophy, but it was an experience that shaped him as a player and as a leader. His story is one of ambition, resilience, and the unwavering belief that success is not always instant—but that, with hard work and determination, it is always within reach.

Chapter 17: The Legacy of a Buccaneer

The Journey of a Buccaneer

As Kabelo Dlamini's career continued to unfold, he began to realize that his time at Orlando Pirates was about more than just winning titles or making a name for himself. It was about creating a legacy—a legacy that would inspire the next generation of players and remind everyone of the power of dedication, hard work, and humility.

Over the years, Kabelo had earned the admiration of fans and teammates alike, not just for his footballing skills but for his commitment to the club and the pride he took in wearing the famous black and white jersey. He had become a symbol of what it meant to be a Buccaneer, and his story—one of perseverance, challenges, and triumphs—was beginning to take on a life of its own.

"There's a feeling that comes with playing for a club like Pirates that's hard to describe," Kabelo says. "It's more than just football. It's about the history, the pride, and the responsibility you carry as a player. You can't take it lightly. You have to give your best every day, because the fans expect nothing less. For me, it's about making them proud and leaving a legacy that will last long after I'm gone."

Kabelo's Influence on the Team

As the years passed, Kabelo's influence on the field grew stronger. His role in the midfield became more pivotal, and his leadership off the pitch was just as important. Over time, he became one of the team's most senior players, a key figure whose experience and calm demeanor were invaluable to the younger players coming through the ranks.

"You start to realize that your role as a senior player goes beyond just what you do on the pitch," Kabelo reflects. "It's about mentoring the younger guys, showing them the way. You're not just playing for yourself anymore—you're playing for the whole team, and you're helping to build something that can stand the test of time."

Kabelo's leadership qualities were never more evident than in moments of adversity. Whether it was a tough loss, an injury, or a period of poor form, Kabelo's ability to keep the team focused and motivated became one of his greatest attributes. His calmness in the face of pressure had a contagious effect, and his commitment to pushing forward inspired those around him to do the same.

"The young players look up to you, and you have a responsibility to show them how to handle the highs and the lows," Kabelo says. "Football isn't just about the good moments. It's about how you respond when things don't go your way. That's when you have to dig deep and show what you're made of."

Contributions Beyond the Pitch

While Kabelo's impact on the pitch was undeniable, his contributions to Orlando Pirates went far beyond the football field. He became a role model for the club's supporters and for young aspiring players, especially from disadvantaged communities like his own in Daveyton. Kabelo's story was one of hope, and it proved that no matter where you came from, with hard work and determination, anything was possible.

In his personal life, Kabelo made it a point to engage with the community, using his platform as a professional footballer to give back. He regularly visited schools, spoke to young players, and participated in various charitable initiatives. For Kabelo, it wasn't enough to just be a successful footballer—he wanted to make a difference in the lives of those who looked up to him.

"I always remember where I come from," Kabelo says. "I remember the struggles of my family, the hardships of growing up in Daveyton. I know that I wouldn't be here without the support of my community. So, I want to give back. I want to show the young people in Daveyton that they too can make it. That's my mission now."

His dedication to helping others was reflected in his involvement with local youth football initiatives, where he mentored young players and helped them navigate the challenges of pursuing a career in football. Kabelo became more than just a role model—he became a beacon of hope for the next generation.

Kabelo's Influence on the Club's Culture

As Kabelo's tenure at Orlando Pirates progressed, his influence extended to shaping the club's culture. His work ethic, discipline, and passion for the game became embedded in the team's ethos. He was an example of what it meant to be a Pirate—dedicated, resilient, and proud of the club's rich history.

The younger players at Pirates began to emulate his professionalism and commitment. Kabelo would often stay behind after training, perfecting his craft and offering advice to anyone who sought it. He led by example, demonstrating that success didn't come without hard work. His efforts were integral in creating a culture of excellence at the club, one where every player, regardless of age or experience, understood the importance of striving for greatness.

"I want the young guys to know that there's no shortcut to success," Kabelo explains. "It's about hard work, consistency, and believing in yourself. Every day is an opportunity to improve, and you can't take that for granted. I've learned that the hard way, and I want to pass that knowledge on to the next generation."

The Bonds with Fans and Teammates

One of the most profound aspects of Kabelo's time at Orlando Pirates was the bond he formed with the fans. From his early days at the club, he had a special connection with the supporters. They admired his humility, his passion for the game, and his unrelenting drive to succeed. Kabelo became a fan favorite, and his name was regularly chanted in the stands at Orlando Stadium.

"The fans are the heart and soul of the club," Kabelo says. "They are the reason we play with so much passion. Every time I step onto that field, I know I'm not just representing myself—I'm representing the entire Pirates nation. The love and support from the fans mean everything to me. It's a privilege to play for them."

Kabelo's relationship with his teammates was equally strong. He had formed deep bonds with his fellow Pirates players, and the camaraderie in the dressing room was a testament to the unity and spirit of the squad. He had learned from some of the best players in the country and had forged friendships that would last a lifetime.

"We're like a family," Kabelo says with a smile. "There's no individualism at Pirates. We win together, we lose together, and we always have each other's backs. That's what makes this club special."

The Next Chapter

As Kabelo's career moved into its later stages, he began to think about life beyond football. He knew that his playing days would eventually come to an end, and when that time came, he wanted to ensure that his legacy would continue to inspire those who came after him.

"I've been blessed to live my dream," Kabelo reflects. "But I also want to make sure that I leave something behind. I want to be remembered not just for what I did on the field, but for how I lived my life. Football is a beautiful game, but it's only a part of who I am.

There's so much more to life, and I want to make a difference in the world beyond football."

Kabelo began to focus on other ventures, including coaching and mentoring young players, and using his platform to continue supporting his community. He also became involved in various business initiatives, determined to create opportunities for himself and others after his football career.

"I want to build a legacy that goes beyond football," Kabelo says. "I want to create opportunities for others, just like I had opportunities given to me. The goal is to leave the world a better place than I found it."

Kabelo's Legacy

Kabelo Dlamini's legacy is one of resilience, determination, and service to others. From his humble beginnings in Daveyton to his rise as one of South Africa's most admired footballers, Kabelo's journey is a testament to the power of hard work and the importance of community. He has become a role model for young players across the country, showing them that with belief and perseverance, anything is possible.

His time at Orlando Pirates may one day come to an end, but his influence on the club, its culture, and the supporters will be felt for years to come. Kabelo's legacy is not just about the goals he scored or the titles he won—it's about the lives he touched and the example he set for the next generation of footballers.

And as he looks toward the future, Kabelo Dlamini remains committed to his mission: to inspire, to give back, and to leave a legacy that will endure long after he hangs up his boots.

Chapter 18: The Legacy in the Making

Kabelo Dlamini's journey is far from over, but when he looks back on all he has accomplished, there's a sense of deep satisfaction. From the streets of Daveyton to the top of South African football, Kabelo has proved time and time again that success is not simply defined by goals scored or matches won—but by the resilience to continue pushing forward, no matter the odds.

At just 28 years old, Kabelo has already experienced more than most could ever dream of. He has played for one of the most iconic clubs in Africa, Orlando Pirates, and contributed to the resurgence of South African football on both the local and continental stage. But his ambition does not stop there. The journey he has taken is not just about the accolades; it's about the lessons learned along the way and the path he's carving for the next generation.

Kabelo's rise to prominence hasn't been easy. He's faced the pressures of balancing expectations from his family, his team, and himself. He's battled injuries, setbacks, and self-doubt. But each of those obstacles has only made him stronger and more determined. He remains an example of perseverance, always striving to better himself—not just as a footballer, but as a man.

Throughout his career, Kabelo has been an advocate for youth development, always stressing the importance of discipline, mindset, and the belief that anyone, regardless of background, can achieve greatness. He continues to give back to his community in Daveyton, ensuring that the next generation of players has the tools to follow in his footsteps. His success has never been about just "making it"; it has always been about inspiring others to reach for their dreams.

As Kabelo looks to the future, his ambitions remain sky-high. He dreams of representing South Africa on the global stage, contributing to the national team's success, and ultimately leading Orlando Pirates to more trophies and victories. But beyond that, he hopes to use the platform his career has given him to make a lasting impact on the next generation—not only in football but in life.

His legacy, while still in the making, is already evident in the way he carries himself, the dedication he puts into his craft, and the way he encourages others to pursue their own dreams. His journey from the dusty streets of Daveyton to the bright lights of Orlando Pirates has been an inspiration to all who have witnessed it.

Kabelo Dlamini is more than a footballer—he is a symbol of hope, a mentor, and a role model. The final chapter of his story is still unwritten, but one thing is certain: he will continue to strive for excellence, break barriers, and create opportunities for those who come after him.

And in the years to come, when new players rise from the streets of South Africa, they will remember the name Kabelo Dlamini—not just for his incredible skills on the field, but for the legacy he has built with every step, every goal, and every challenge overcome.

The journey is ongoing, and Kabelo Dlamini's best chapters are yet to be written.

Chapter 19: The Road Still to Travel

A Career Defined by Struggles and Triumphs

Kabelo Dlamini's journey through football is still unfolding. As he reflects on where he is now—a key player for Orlando Pirates, one of South Africa's most celebrated clubs—he knows the road ahead remains long, filled with opportunities, challenges, and tests of character. The victories, the accolades, and the spotlight have all come his way, but for Kabelo, they are not the defining moments of his career. It is the journey itself—the quiet moments of self-doubt, the sacrifices made in the name of passion, the endless hours spent perfecting his craft—that have truly shaped him.

Every footballer has dreams, but it is the relentless pursuit of those dreams, even when the odds seem stacked against you, that truly sets the best apart. Kabelo's rise from the dusty streets of Daveyton to the hallowed grounds of Orlando Pirates is a testament to the power of belief, discipline, and perseverance. His story is not just one of success in the footballing world but of how far a determined soul can go when they refuse to give up.

A Dream Not Yet Realized

Though Kabelo's achievements have brought him respect and admiration, there is one goal he continues to chase: a call-up to the national team, Bafana Bafana. As of yet, that dream has not been realized. But Kabelo remains undeterred. His drive to play for his country is unwavering. He has seen other talented South African players don the national jersey, and he knows that his time will come if he continues to put in the work.

"I'm not looking for shortcuts," Kabelo says with conviction. "I know what it takes to earn my place. I'll keep pushing, keep proving that I belong. That's all I can do."

The world of football is filled with uncertainties. Injury, competition, and fluctuating form can derail even the most promising careers. But Kabelo's focus remains clear. He isn't waiting for an invitation. He is actively shaping his future, one match at a time.

"I know the call-up will come when I've done everything I can to prove that I deserve it," Kabelo reflects. "I won't stop until I get there, because playing for my country is the greatest honor I could ever have."

The Drive for Excellence

Kabelo's journey has always been defined by an intrinsic drive for excellence. His ability to stand out in the competitive environment of South African football is a direct result of his relentless work ethic and commitment to improvement. Training never stops for him—every day is another chance to grow, to get better, to evolve.

But his growth isn't just about physical skills. Kabelo has learned to refine his mental game. The challenges he faced early in his career—being overlooked, fighting for recognition, overcoming setbacks—have all strengthened his resolve. In a sport where the line between success and failure is often razor-thin, Kabelo has learned to embrace the pressure. Every game is an opportunity, and every challenge is a lesson.

"I've been through a lot," Kabelo admits. "I've had my ups and downs, just like anyone. But every failure, every tough moment, just made me stronger. It taught me how to fight, how to stay focused, how to never give up."

The Strength of Support

Throughout his career, Kabelo has been guided not just by his own resolve but by the unwavering support of those closest to him. His family, his coaches, and his teammates have all played pivotal roles in his development. From his days as a young boy in Daveyton, playing street football, to his time at Orlando Pirates, Kabelo has always had a strong support system that believes in him.

"My family has been my rock," Kabelo says. "They've always believed in me, even when I had doubts. Every step of the way, they've been there, pushing me to do my best, to aim higher, and to never settle for less."

But it hasn't just been family. His coaches, particularly those like Siyangaphi and Musa Nyatama, shaped his understanding of the game. They showed him that football is more than just skill—it's about discipline, attitude, and a willingness to learn.

"I owe a lot to the coaches who believed in me and helped me grow," Kabelo reflects. "They didn't just teach me football. They taught me how to be a professional, how to manage myself off the pitch, and how to be a leader."

The Challenge of Staying Hungry

Now, at the peak of his career, Kabelo finds himself at a crossroads. Many players, after achieving so much, begin to lose their edge. They become complacent, satisfied with what they've accomplished. But for Kabelo, the fire is still burning. If anything, his journey has only deepened his hunger for success.

"I'm not done yet," Kabelo says, the intensity in his voice palpable. "I'm always looking for the next step, the next challenge. I want to keep improving, keep growing. There's always more to do."

This mindset has made him not only a great player but also a great leader. He leads by example, pushing his teammates to excel, showing them what it means to never stop working, never stop striving for greatness. He is the player who stays late after practice, the one who holds himself to the highest standards, and the one who demands the same of those around him.

"I've learned that it's not just about being good," Kabelo says. "It's about pushing others to be good, too. A team is only as strong as its weakest player, and it's my responsibility to help lift everyone up."

The Ultimate Goal: Legacy

As Kabelo looks ahead, he is acutely aware of the legacy he wants to leave behind. He is not concerned with fleeting fame or short-term glory. What matters most to him is the impact he will have on the game, the lessons he will pass on to the next generation, and the inspiration he will provide to young footballers back in Daveyton, who look to him as a symbol of what is possible.

"My legacy will be about more than just goals and assists," Kabelo says. "It's about showing that with hard work, determination, and belief in yourself, anything is possible. If I can inspire one kid from my neighborhood to chase their dreams, to believe in themselves like I believed in myself, then I'll have done my job."

The road ahead is still filled with unknowns, but Kabelo faces it with the same resilience that has defined his career. His dream of playing for Bafana Bafana is still alive, and his journey toward greatness is still unfolding. One thing is certain: Kabelo Dlamini will continue to work, to strive, and to grow, pushing the limits of his potential every day.

And when the final chapter of his footballing career is written, Kabelo knows that his story will be one of perseverance, passion, and the relentless pursuit of dreams—a story that will inspire generations to come.

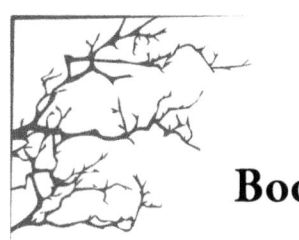

Book Description

Shuffle: The Rise of Kabelo Dlamini is an inspiring story of passion, perseverance, and purpose. Born in the vibrant streets of Daveyton, Kabelo Dlamini—known as "Shuffle"—defied the odds to rise from humble beginnings to becoming one of South Africa's most promising football stars.

This book takes you on a journey through Kabelo's life, from his first steps into football, playing in dusty township fields, to his rise through local clubs and trials at professional academies. Experience his challenges, triumphs, and growth as he transitions to Bloemfontein Celtic, earns a spot in the Orlando Pirates squad, and pursues his dream of representing South Africa on the global stage.

Packed with lessons of hard work, discipline, and resilience, this story highlights the sacrifices made by his family, the guidance of influential mentors, and the unshakable belief in the power of dreams.

Shuffle: The Rise of Kabelo Dlamini is more than just a sports biography—it's a celebration of hope, dedication, and the relentless pursuit of greatness. A must-read for football fans, dreamers, and anyone seeking inspiration to overcome life's challenges.

Don't miss out!

Visit the website below and you can sign up to receive emails whenever Sibusiso Anthon Mkhwanazi publishes a new book. There's no charge and no obligation.

https://books2read.com/r/B-A-QNVAB-TXHOF

BOOKS 2 READ

Connecting independent readers to independent writers.

Also by Sibusiso Anthon Mkhwanazi

Million-Dollar Decade
Resilience Beyond Pain
Resonance Of Hope
Cheating hearts to true love
The Dream Builders Of Daveyton
Before the Bible
Ink and Imagination
Becoming A Millionaire In South Africa
Leaders of the World
Mining In Africa
Origins of Language and Civilization
Vita Nova Centre
Sisters of A cursed bloodline
Witchcraft in Africa
Ghosts of the golden city
Connected Hearts
Lost in Tokyo found in you
A man of many homes
Shuffle: The Rise of Kabelo Dlamini

About the Author

Sibusiso Anthon Mkhwanazi is a versatile and dynamic author from Daveyton, South Africa. Known for his ability to navigate multiple genres with ease, his writing captures the complexities of human experiences, blending heartfelt emotion, gripping narratives, and vivid storytelling.

Sibusiso's work spans crime fiction, romance, poetry, and motivational writing. He is the creative force behind several upcoming books, including Sisters of a Cursed Bloodline, Under the Roof There is No Money: A Millionaire's Journey, and Shuffle: The Rise of Kabelo Dlamini. His stories often explore themes of resilience, love, family dynamics, and the pursuit of success, resonating deeply with readers.

Inspired by his own journey, Sibusiso also writes about the challenges and triumphs of life in South Africa. From tales of hardship to uplifting narratives of self-made success, his work reflects the vibrancy and struggles of his community. His romance novel Lost in

Tokyo, Found in You beautifully weaves love and adventure, set against the backdrop of one of the world's most iconic cities.

Sibusiso's passion for storytelling began in his youth and has blossomed into a career as a multi-genre author. When he's not writing, he works as a cleaner for Tsebo Cleaning Solutions at Botshelong Hospital, drawing inspiration from the resilience of everyday people.

Through his diverse projects, Sibusiso Anthon Mkhwanazi is fast becoming a compelling voice in South African literature, committed to creating stories that entertain, inspire, and empower.